Strong Women Quotes

100 Lines, Sayings, Quotes for Strong Women

THE GRUMPY GURU

The Grumpy Guru

Printed in the United States of America

First Printing, 2018

ISBN: 9781983101908

http://thegrumpy.guru
http://365ways.me

This book is dedicated to all of you strong people who are taking responsibility of your own feelings and doing something to be better.

All my heartfelt gratitude to the following people: my mom Ruby Jane, you have made me everything I am today; my dad Nestor-- my eternal, my angel, and the source of my perseverance; Mommyling, my spiritual guide ; Ria & Joe, the true witnesses of my transformation and my foundation pillars; Ellie Jane, the sparkle of our eyes;

Juan, thanks for always encouraging me to push harder - you are my ONE; Rocco & Radha, my reason for everything.

The Love of my family and friends is the fountain of inspiration that never runs dry. Thank you for constantly inspiring me, motivating me, and loving me unconditionally.

This book will never be complete without the help of my trusted and talented friends, Roillan James Paña, and everyone at NOW for the moral support.

For reals, I am sick of Chicken Soup! It's not all rainbows and puppies in this world.

I put together a collection of various works to help me find inner strength and peace. I realized that sometimes we just need a real version of ways to feel better and go on with our daily lives.

I am The Grumpy Guru and I know grumpy more than the average grump. I realized that for whatever I am feeling, I had the power to switch to a more positive disposition with a little bit of guidance, a little bit of insight and a line or 2 of text.

I don't think I'll ever stop being grumpy but with the help of these snippets, I can channel them in a positive direction. If this works for me, I can only hope it will work for most people.

This is The Grumpy Guru's take to tackle and manage moments of darkness, doubt, and insecurity.

It's OK to be a grumpy, but Grumps can be Blissfully Happy, too.

I suggest you read what touches you, what helps you move on and what works for you. I've given you 365 different ways and it's up to you what you want to read in this book.

Trust me in my 41 years of grumpiness, I'm still here managing and coping and being relatively happy & content.

Cheers to you guys!

THE GRUMPY GURU

Let's All Be Blissfully Grumpy Together

A powerful woman is in charge of her destiny without losing her identity. Her strength comes from her security in her femininity and empowering others to live and find meaning to what they are called to do in this life. You are a Strong Woman and this is your reminder.

The Grumpy Guru

\\

A strong woman
carries herself with
firmness despite
all the chaos
within.

//

\\

A strong woman combines both steel and velvet. She knows where to stand and she knows when to submit.

//

\\

God fashioned
women to
complement men.
She knows where
here strength lies.

//

\\

A strong woman doesn't carry a victim mentality. She may have her share of vulnerability in the past but she was able to find herself along the way. She learned to be the alpha that she is.

//

\\

A strong woman's
true strength is
her faith.

//

\\

A genuinely strong woman is not insecure when others are much better than hers. She knows her worth and never walks away from it.

//

\\

A strong woman
things of others
before herself
because she
knows that life is
not just about her.

//

\\

A strong woman
knows her worth.
She is unselfish
and infuses life
to others to
give hope.

//

\\

She's not easily swayed by the hectic schedules of life. She takes times for herself.

//

\\

Powerful women
freely loves.
They act based
on love and are
determined to
love despite of.

//

\\

Your walk may be slow but it doesn't mean you're out of the race.

//

\\

She recognizes counsel and seeks help to those whose opinion matters even if means hurting her ego.

//

\\

Strong women deal with issues logically and emotionally. She's a balance of steel and velvet.

//

\\

A strong woman doesn't curb to the hurt. She falls down but she never stays there for very long.

//

\\

A strong woman
knows how to
value her body.
She is what
she eats.

//

\\

A strong woman has a sense of humor. She knows her flaws and doesn't mind a joke or two hurled her way.

//

\\

A strong woman
handles issues
with wit, humor
and wisdom.

//

\\

A strong woman is a life long learner. She doesn't let her past get in the way of her future.

//

\\

Powerful women listen to counsel. They know how to discern wisdom even if it contradicts her stance if it is for the betterment personally or for others.

//

\\

Insecure women wants to be heard. Strong women are naturally heard.

//

\\

Powerful women don't force their ideas on others. She is the one that people turns to for advice.

//

\\

Powerful
women have
self-confidence
but not arrogance.

//

\\

Strong women
have the power
to accomplish
great things.

//

\\

She is not afraid
of the hurdles
that comes with
challenges.

//

\\

A strong woman develops a go-getter mindset. She's always waiting to strike when opportunity arrives.

//

\\

Strong women
plan for the future.
She's secure in her
abilities and
knows her value.

//

\\

A strong woman
is confident.
People are
naturally drawn
to her in more
circumstances
beyond beauty
and brains.

//

\\

Strong women are
intense in their
passions. She sets
high standards
for herself.

//

\\

Strong women set life standards that shows in how she lives her life.

//

\\

What sets a
powerful woman
to a mediocre one
is their standards
and passion.
She's secure in her
abilities to deliver
her craft.

//

\\

Strong women are not afraid to lay out judgements and still not be judgemental. They are winsome in stating their case without belittling others.

//

\\

They are not afraid
to fail. They are just
afraid by not trying
hard enough.

//

\\

For a strong
woman, to return
exhausted from
battle is better
than not trying
at all.

//

\\

Sitting on her laurels
is not an option.
A strong women
is in pursuit of
progress within
and outside herself.

//

\\

She is happy in
her disposition.
She carries a
cheerful heart.

//

\\

Strong women are not afraid of change. She knows that it is an opportunity disguised as an impossible task.

//

\\

Strong women assume responsibility with their decisions.

//

\\

A strong woman
is mature in
her decisions.
She doesn't
takes all into
considerations
even if it meant
denying herself
of comfort.

//

\\

While majority are
looking to fit in,
the strong woman
looks to strive
for greatness.

//

\\

She fears
mediocrity more
than she fears
change.

//

\\

She finds contentment in progress. Strong women know that mediocrity is being untrue to oneself.

//

\\

Powerful women are able to break through the bondage of mediocrity and experience the liberation of greatness.

//

\\

She's not limited to her circumstances. A powerful woman lives in boundless possibilities.

//

\\

She doesn't waste her life settling for anything less.

//

\\

A powerful woman sees vision. A mediocre woman settles for what's comfortable.

//

\\

Strong women are often seen as unrealistic. But when she shoots for the stars, the universe follows.

//

\\

Powerful women are naturally drawn to their kind. She's not the one to associate with mediocre people.

//

\\

Powerful women overflow with optimism and possibilities.

//

\\

Strong women know they are a genius in their own right. They are not resigned to mediocrity.

//

\\

Strong woman takes the road less traveled and follow their dreams.

//

\\

Powerful women oozes with enthusiasm when it comes to their vision in life.

//

\\

Powerful women are constantly battling with anything less than excellent.

//

\\

Strong women live above average lives. There's are always new things to explore and they see the best in what lies ahead.

//

\\

They cultivate an optimistic mind and stay away from negative crowds.

//

\\

They light up the room when they enter instead of when they leave.

//

\\

Strong women don't accept things the way they are just because society says so.

//

\\

Strong women
believes in the
good in others.

//

\\

Strong women are highly committed in their endeavors. They either get it or keep trying.

//

\\

Successful women always surrounds herself with wise counsels. She's not afraid to find people who contradicts her opinions.

//

\\

Powerful women knows how to set time-bounded and realistic goals. She shoots for stars but she takes it one step at a time.

//

\\

Strong women have an intense desire to keep reading. She knows it helps her to understand the world better.

//

\\

Passionate women are intense in their endeavors. They will keep acquiring knowledge to develop their skills.

//

\\

Women who are passionate about life knows that the only way up is to keep climbing higher.

//

\\

She carries with
her a powerful
mindset enough
to bring light
to a whole room
of gloom.

//

\\

A strong woman
is always
battle ready.

//

\\

She doesn't want
like a shifting
shadow. She stays
on her course until
she sees the end
of her voyage.

//

\\

Strong women
plays it cool when
someone jabs
a malicious
comment. She
knows how to time
her words well.

//

\\

If she makes a mistake, she owns it. A strong woman learns from this experience and moves forward.

//

\\

A strong woman carries herself with dignity and pride.

//

\\

A strong woman
helps others
even if means
sacrificing her
comfort for the
benefit of others.

//

\\

A strong woman
sees the days
of her life with
care and love.

//

\\

Powerful women
have optimism
that can generate
hope in a nation.

//

\\

Powerful women
knows when to use
power and when
to give power.

//

\\

Passionate women
take good care
of themselves.
They grow in
age gracefully.

//

\\

Powerful women knows how when to accept situations and be flexible.

//

\\

Her confidence is not feeble. Her resolve is sure as her faith is secure.

//

\\

She's constant
in her intensity
and goals in life.

//

\\

A strong woman does not act on first impulse. She analyzes the situation before taking any actions.

//

\\

She's sure in her goals but flexible in her steps.

//

\\

A powerful woman
does not make
an idol of her
relationship. She's a
single person IN a
relationship.

//

\\

She's an equal
to her mate.
She's secure in
her status and
supports
her partner.

//

\\

A mediocre woman needs constant attention. A strong woman is sought for guidance.

//

\\

She's financially independent.

//

\\

She can take
care of her needs
without having
to depend on
her partner
for support.

//

\\

She draws energy
from within not
from others.

//

\\

Within a strong
lies a steadfast
love for her
people.

//

\\

Strong women
know who they are.
They are not
embarrassed
to show their
true selves.

//

\\

Powerful women may grow in wisdom but they stay true to themselves.

//

\\

Strong women stick it out when they see a cause worth fighting for.

//

\\

Powerful women seeks to pave the way for the next generation.

//

\\

Strong women
always take the
initiative to
keep growing.

//

\\

Despite what they believe in, strong women always leave room for improvement.

//

\\

Strong women are teachers and students at the same time. They know when to teach and they know when to listen and learn.

//

\\

Strong women are not limited by their niche industry. They know that building relationships outside work can help and balance other interests.

//

\\

They are on the constant look out for opportunities to diversify their skills, relationships and partnerships.

//

\\

Strong women are often inquisitive with everything going around them.

//

\\

Strong women
are not afraid
to question the
norms. If they
see something
that needs
improvement,
they will work on it.

//

\\

Strong women embraces all her emotions. She is genuine in dealing with issues with grace and wisdom.

//

\\

Honesty is the most valued trait of a strong woman.

//

\\

A strong woman
values others worth
just as she does
with hers.

//

Other Titles By
The Grumpy Guru

Quotes About Changing
Success Quotes
Motivation Quotes
Marriage Quotes
Dog Quotes
Boyfriend Quotes
Happiness Quotes
Quotes for Teachers
Inspiring Quotes
What A Life Quotes
Family Quotes
On Love Quotes
Best Friend Quotes
Quotes Friendship
Beach Quotes
Quotes for Life
Encouragement Quotes
Teamwork Quotes

Book Ordering

To order your copy / copies of
Strong Women Quotes:
100 Lines, Sayings, Quotes for Strong Women

by The Grumpy Guru,
please visit: thegrumpy.guru.

You can also check out other titles
available.

Bulk Pricing and
Affiliate Programs Available

Printed in Great Britain
by Amazon